the fishes Beneath Tropic Seas

ISBN 0-913008 18 4

Text and artwork by Idaz Greenberg

Design and layout by Idaz Greenberg

Photographs by Jerry and Michael Greenberg

Copyright © 1986, 1987 Jerry, Idaz and Michael Greenberg

Published by SEAHAWK PRESS All rights reserved

6840 S.W. 92 Street, Miami, Florida 33156 U.S.A.

Fish-finder

Cover, Blue angelfish photo by Jerry Greenberg

Blue tang, left   Roughhead blenny, above   Photos by Michael Greenberg

Morays

As beautiful and repulsive as the snakes they resemble, these fish have smooth, scaleless skin. Narrow, muscular jaws can drive the fanglike teeth deeply into anything they grasp. The bite itself is not toxic, but since the teeth invariably are contaminated with decayed food particles, serious infection may follow if the wound is not treated. Largely nocturnal and secretive by nature, morays hide in crevices and under coral ledges. They are generally harmless to man unless provoked. Morays should never be eaten, since some individuals of all species are capable of causing severe food poisoning, or even death.

Photos by Jerry Greenberg

3 **Spotted moray** *(Gymnothorax moringa)* This moray is usually found in shallow water coral and rock areas. It may grow to four feet.

4 **Viper moray** *(Enchelycore nigricans)* Strongly arched jaws expose the many awesome teeth of the viper moray even when the mouth is closed. This eel ranges up to three feet long.

5 **Purplemouth moray** *(Gymnothorax vicinus)* Varying in body color from a nearly uniform brown to a densely-mottled pattern, the purplemouth may grow to four feet. The dark purplish color inside the lower jaw contrasts with pale lavender at the roof.

1 **Green moray** *(Gymnothorax funebris)* This species reaches the greatest size of Atlantic morays, more than six feet. The green color is the result of a yellowish mucus overlaying the dark blue skin.

2 **Goldentail moray** *(Muraena miliaris)* A small moray not exceeding two feet, the goldentail moray has tiny teeth even for its size. The attractive yellow markings vary greatly, but the golden color is most extensive and pronounced at the tail tip.

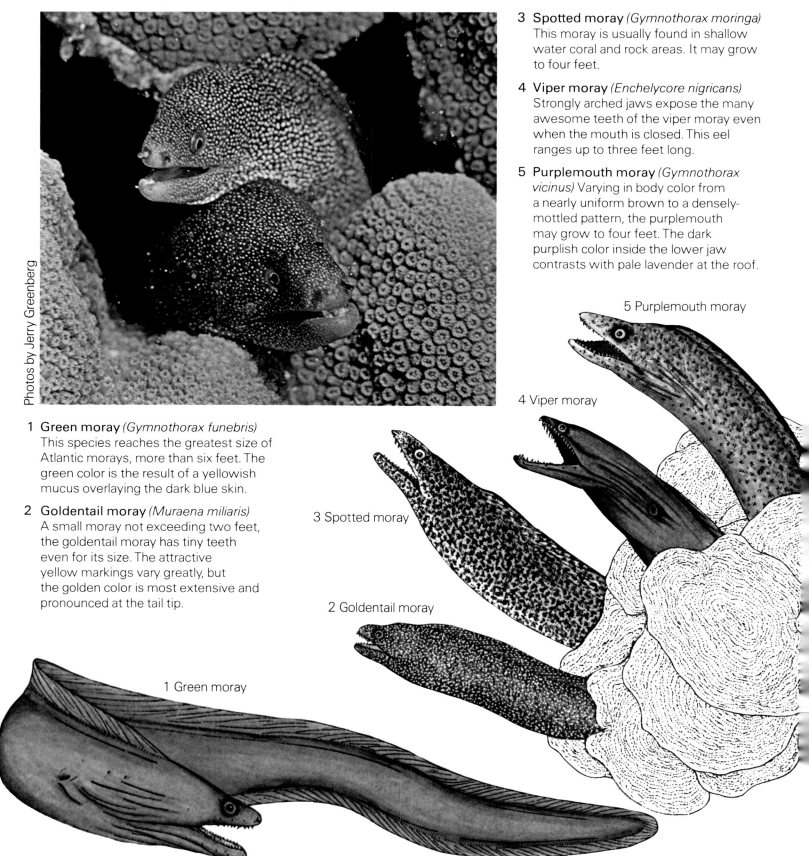

5 Purplemouth moray

4 Viper moray

3 Spotted moray

2 Goldentail moray

1 Green moray

2

Goldentail moray, left and above

Redspotted hawkfish

Photos by Jerry Greenberg

Glassy sweepers

Gobies

Bright markings on these two-inch gobies attract other fish to the cleaning stations set up by them. Gobies gain a free meal of parasites for the service.

1 **Neon goby** *(Gobiosoma oceanops)*
3 **Cleaning goby** *(Gobiosoma genie)*
4 **Sharknose goby** *(Gobiosoma evelynae)*

2 **Bridled goby** *(Coryphopterus glauco-fraenum)* burrows its translucent body in sandy bottom. Size is three inches.

Jawfish

5 **Yellowhead jawfish** *(Opistognathus aurifrons)* turns slowly above its burrow, feeding on small organisms passing by. Length is almost four inches.

Blenny

6 **Redlip blenny** *(Ophioblennius atlanticus)* may grow to almost five inches.

Sweeper

7 **Glassy sweeper** *(Pempheris schomburgki)* lends a coppery luster to the caves and hollows it inhabits. Size is six inches.

Hawkfish

8 **Redspotted hawkfish** *(Amblycirrhitus pinos)* often balances on its pectoral fins over coral. Size reached is less than four inches.

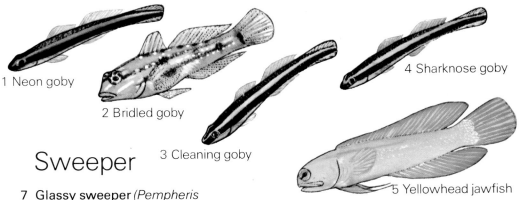

1 Neon goby
2 Bridled goby
3 Cleaning goby
4 Sharknose goby
5 Yellowhead jawfish

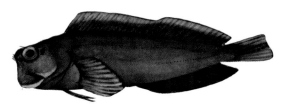

6 Redlip blenny

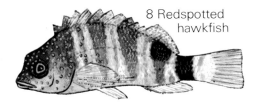

8 Redspotted hawkfish

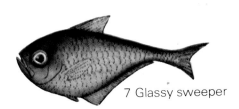

7 Glassy sweeper

Adult male stoplight parrotfish

Photo by Jerry Greenberg

Parrotfishes

With teeth fused together into parrotlike beaks and heavy molar grinding bones in the throat, parrotfishes are efficient recycling machines, turning coral and rock into fine sand as they graze on algae and polyps. Parrotfishes often form large schools of several different species, all rowing along with their pectoral fins in the same style as wrasses. They are daytime feeders.

At night, some appear to go to sleep under ledges and in caves. Here, they secrete protective mucous coccoons in which they wrap themselves until morning. Females and males of most species have different color patterns, with the adult males gaudiest. Species having similarly colored sexes occasionally produce larger and more brilliantly colored terminal-phase males or "supermales." Parrotfish flesh spoils quickly and blue parrotfish is sometimes poisonous.

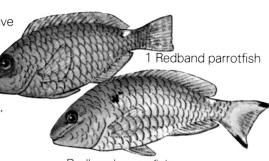

1 Redband parrotfish

Redband parrotfish

1 **Redband parrotfish** *(Sparisoma aurofrenatum)* are small, reaching about 11 inches. The white tail saddle is distinctive, as are the dark markings on the adult male.

2 **Stoplight parrotfish** *(Sparisoma viride)* Note the round yellow spot on the gill cover and the yellow tail base on the adult male. Red-phase individuals are unmistakable. Size reached is 20 inches.

3 **Queen parrotfish** *(Scarus vetula)* Drab-phase males and females differ from the adult male in both color and tail shape. Adult males grow to two feet.

4 **Blue parrotfish** *(Scarus coeruleus)* Large adults (perhaps only males) develop a hump on the forehead. They are said to reach a length of up to four feet.

5 **Striped parrotfish** *(Scarus croicensis)* grows to less than one foot.

6 **Midnight parrotfish** *(Scarus coelestinus)* feature green teeth, as do the rainbow parrotfish. Size reached is 30 inches.

7 **Princess parrotfish** *(Scarus taeniopterus)* Note the yellow mid-body blotch on the adult male. Size is about 13 inches.

8 **Rainbow parrotfish** *(Scarus guacamaia)* Adult males may grow to four feet and are extremely heavy-bodied.

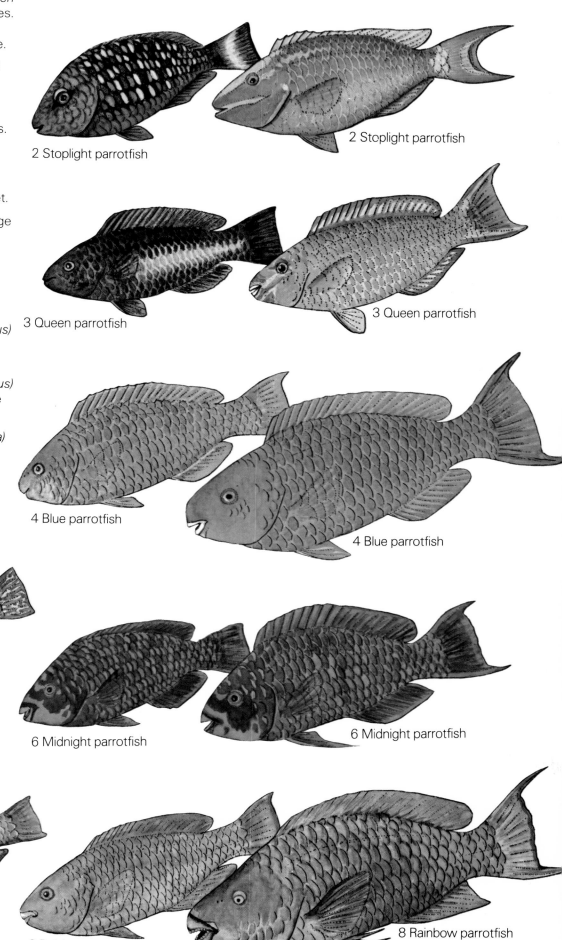

2 Stoplight parrotfish

2 Stoplight parrotfish

3 Queen parrotfish

3 Queen parrotfish

4 Blue parrotfish

4 Blue parrotfish

5 Striped parrotfish

5 Striped parrotfish

6 Midnight parrotfish

6 Midnight parrotfish

7 Princess parrotfish

7 Princess parrotfish

8 Rainbow parrotfish

8 Rainbow parrotfish

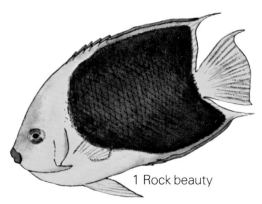

1 Rock beauty

Rock beauty
juvenile

Angelfishes

Angelfishes are the most curious fish on the reef. Their often gaudy colors blend in surprisingly well as they flutter among sea fans or nibble on bright-hued sponges. Immature angels, marked with color patterns different from adults, sometimes augment their diet with parasites they remove from other fish.

1 **Rock beauty** *(Holacanthus tricolor)* The discus-shaped body features a dark spot that increases in size as the fish grows to its ultimate length of one foot.

Photos by Jerry Greenberg

Spanish hogfish, left

Rock beauty, above

Angelfishes continued

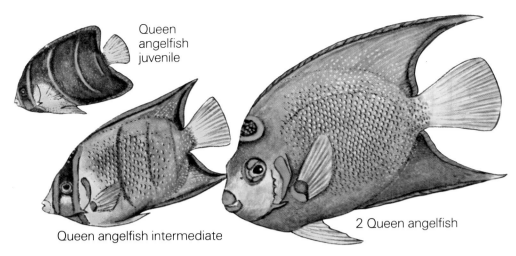

Queen angelfish juvenile

Queen angelfish intermediate

2 Queen angelfish

2 **Queen angelfish** *(Holacanthus ciliaris)* Garbed in a galaxy of colors, the queen angelfish derives its imperial status from the blue-ringed crown on its nape, above the eyes. The queen is distinguished from the similar blue angelfish by its crown, yellow-rimmed scales and all-yellow tail. Juveniles are also similar to those of the blue angelfish, but the last major vertical bar is always curved on the body. Both angelfishes grow to 18 inches.

Blue angelfish

3 **Blue angelfish** *(Holacanthus bermudensis),* despite rich coloring, appears as a poor relation to the queen angelfish. Tan with blue and white highlights, it lacks the queen's crown and its tail is merely bordered with yellow. In juveniles, the last major vertical bar is a straight line although it may curve where it extends onto the fins. Blue and queen angelfishes hybridize and produce specimens with intermediate color patterns in the Florida Keys and Bahamas.

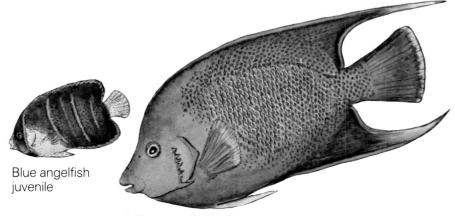

Blue angelfish juvenile

3 Blue angelfish

Queen angelfish

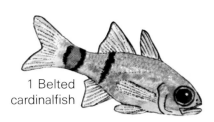
1 Belted cardinalfish

2 Flamefish

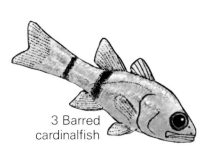
3 Barred cardinalfish

Belted cardinalfish

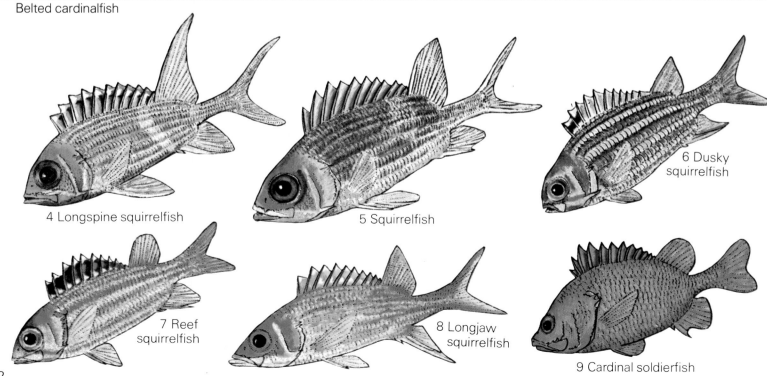
4 Longspine squirrelfish

5 Squirrelfish

6 Dusky squirrelfish

7 Reef squirrelfish

8 Longjaw squirrelfish

9 Cardinal soldierfish

Cardinalfishes

1 **Belted cardinalfish** *(Apogon townsendi)* This tiny iridescent fish grows to almost three inches. Males incubate eggs orally.

2 **Flamefish** *(Apogon maculatus)* Large black eyes striped with white and black interrupt the vivid red on the five-inch flamefish.

3 **Barred cardinalfish** *(Apogon binotatus)* Ranging from red to pallid in hue, two narrow black bars remain constant to distinguish this fish, which reaches five inches.

Squirrelfishes

4 **Longspine squirrelfish** *(Holocentrus rufus)* Marked with white spots near the margin of its spiny dorsal fin, this fish grows to over one foot.

5 **Squirrelfish** *(Holocentrus ascensionis)* The golden orange dorsal fin separates this 15-inch fish from its look-alike, the longspine squirrelfish.

6 **Dusky squirrelfish** *(Holocentrus vexillarius)* A broad black stripe between the first and third dorsal fin spines mark this six-inch squirrelfish. The dark red and white stripes on the upper half of the body are separated by fine black lines.

7 **Reef squirrelfish** *(Holocentrus coruscus)* The first three or four dorsal fin spines are marked by a black spot with whitish borders above and below. These black spots continue as a red stripe farther back on this small (5.5 inches) squirrelfish.

8 **Longjaw squirrelfish** *(Holocentrus marianus)* A projecting lower jaw and long anal fin spine that can reach to the tail base characterizes this eight-inch fish.

9 **Cardinal soldierfish** *(Plectrypops retrospinis)* This fish is all red. It grows to five inches.

10 **Blackbar soldierfish** *(Myripristis jacobus)* Named for the dark bar behind its head, the blackbar soldierfish can grow to eight inches.

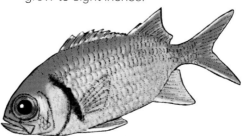

10 Blackbar soldierfish

Longspine squirrelfish

Photos by Jerry Greenberg

Squirrelfish are generally considered edible, but their small size and spiny, prickly bodies discourage most people from eating them.

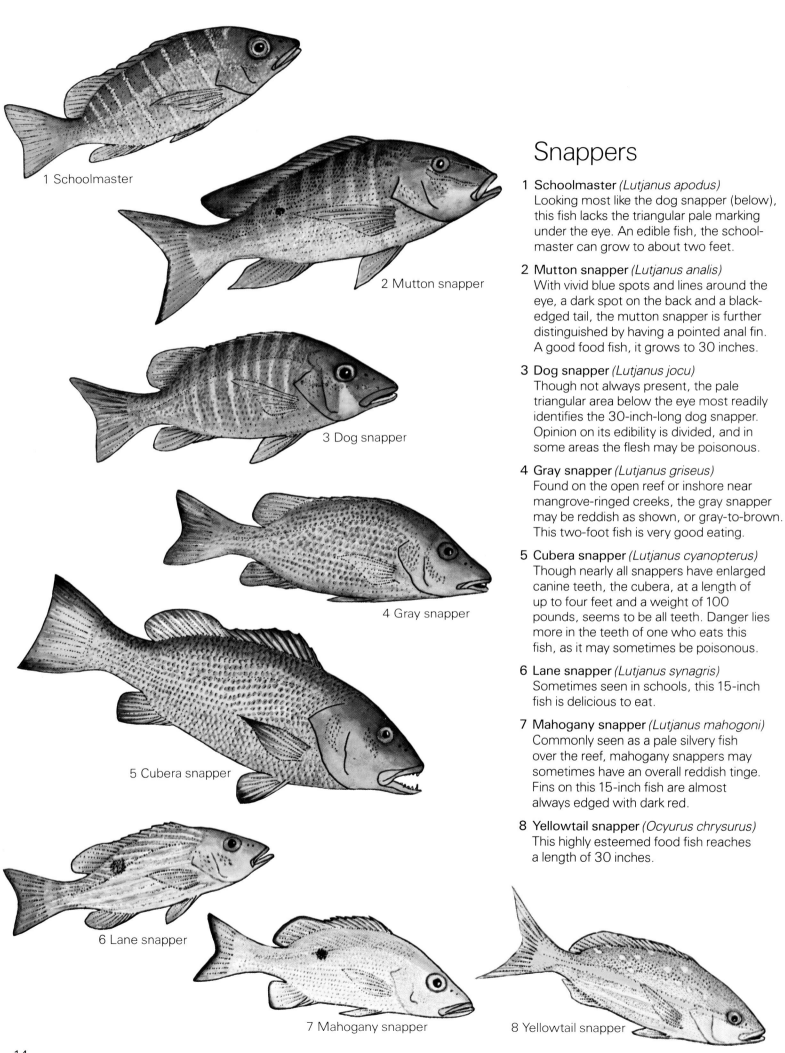

1 Schoolmaster

2 Mutton snapper

3 Dog snapper

4 Gray snapper

5 Cubera snapper

6 Lane snapper

7 Mahogany snapper

8 Yellowtail snapper

Snappers

1 **Schoolmaster** *(Lutjanus apodus)*
Looking most like the dog snapper (below), this fish lacks the triangular pale marking under the eye. An edible fish, the school-master can grow to about two feet.

2 **Mutton snapper** *(Lutjanus analis)*
With vivid blue spots and lines around the eye, a dark spot on the back and a black-edged tail, the mutton snapper is further distinguished by having a pointed anal fin. A good food fish, it grows to 30 inches.

3 **Dog snapper** *(Lutjanus jocu)*
Though not always present, the pale triangular area below the eye most readily identifies the 30-inch-long dog snapper. Opinion on its edibility is divided, and in some areas the flesh may be poisonous.

4 **Gray snapper** *(Lutjanus griseus)*
Found on the open reef or inshore near mangrove-ringed creeks, the gray snapper may be reddish as shown, or gray-to-brown. This two-foot fish is very good eating.

5 **Cubera snapper** *(Lutjanus cyanopterus)*
Though nearly all snappers have enlarged canine teeth, the cubera, at a length of up to four feet and a weight of 100 pounds, seems to be all teeth. Danger lies more in the teeth of one who eats this fish, as it may sometimes be poisonous.

6 **Lane snapper** *(Lutjanus synagris)*
Sometimes seen in schools, this 15-inch fish is delicious to eat.

7 **Mahogany snapper** *(Lutjanus mahogoni)*
Commonly seen as a pale silvery fish over the reef, mahogany snappers may sometimes have an overall reddish tinge. Fins on this 15-inch fish are almost always edged with dark red.

8 **Yellowtail snapper** *(Ocyurus chrysurus)*
This highly esteemed food fish reaches a length of 30 inches.

Gray snappers

Photo by Jerry Greenberg